I0160713

Fighting for Truth

**A Trial Lawyer's Insight Into
What It Takes To Win.**

David W Holub

Foreword by Rob Anspach

David W Holub

Fighting For Truth: A Trial Lawyer's Insight Into What It Takes To Win.

Copyright © 2018 by Anspach Media and David W. Holub

All rights reserved. No part of this book may be reproduced or transmitted in any form or by any means without written permission from the author.

ISBN 10: 1-7324682-0-6
ISBN 13: 978-1-7324682-0-7

Printed in USA

Disclaimer: This book is designed to give the reader general information on the legal subjects contained herein. It is offered with the understanding that the author and publisher do not guarantee any specific future results. The author is not rendering legal or other professional advice on specific facts or matters and, accordingly, assumes no liability whatsoever in connection with its use. *Information about a previous success IN NO WAY is to be considered predictive of similar success in the future, nor be taken to create an expectation that similar results can be achieved in the future.* No court has approved any aspect of this writing nor endorsed any portion of the content of this writing. The matters discussed by the author involve Indiana law and no effort is made to consider the laws of other states or nations

About Confidentiality

The case information noted in this book reflects only information contained in public records. No non-public information about any case is revealed. Further, to maintain privacy and confidentiality, no case identifying information is provided.

All proceeds generated by this book will go to one or more of the charitable entities identified on the "service" page of our website.

To RCV and KCVH.

David W Holub

"I believe that unarmed truth and unconditional love will have the final word in reality. This is why right, temporarily defeated, is stronger than evil triumphant."

- Martin Luther King, Jr.

David W Holub

Table of Contents

David W Holub

Foreword

A few years ago, I received a phone call. That phone call has turned into a friendship. The person calling me was David Holub, an Indiana Personal Injury Trial Attorney.

Now you might be thinking, "okay, and…"

Well, David is not just an ordinary attorney. He's actually Batman. No seriously…David is part detective, part hero, part technology gadget man and an advocate for helping people recover from the wrongs done to them by others.

What sets David apart, from others in his field, is that he's not afraid to go into the court arena and battle it out with insurance companies. He's not one to take the easy path and accept a settlement offer if he knows a jury will award more.

Nope, not your typical lawyer.

David takes the time to educate potential clients with YouTube videos, blog articles and even social media.

And he's always warning people that although social media is great for keeping in touch with friends and family, it's not a good idea to talk about or post pictures of your injury before or during a case.

So, if you would like to know what a Trial Lawyer does, or how a Trial Lawyer can help you, then this book is a great guide.

David peppers each chapter with stories, anecdotes and lessons to give you, the reader, a deeper insight into what is involved in preparing and taking a case before a jury.

Trust me, you will enjoy this book.

Rob Anspach

Introduction

Why read this book?

It's a fair question. As a trial lawyer, most of my time is spent either in the courtroom or doing the work that makes for success in the courtroom. Such as questioning witnesses and researching the law. But unless I bring you into the courtroom with me, how can I explain what it is like to battle things out in the courtroom? If you were my client, I could of course take you into the courtroom with me, but I handle personal injury cases mainly, and I wouldn't wish an injury on anyone, but if you ever need my services this book describes what it is like preparing for battle behind the scenes and heading into the courtroom with a trial lawyer.

In short then, this book gives you a glimpse of what it takes to prepare to win at trial, and pulls you into the courtroom, but it doesn't pull you in very deep. It is not a skills book for lawyers. It is rather a book for lay people similar to what you might expect from a surgeon explaining what it's like to perform surgery, without the bloody details, or the boring chapters about the years in medical school.

What's in it for you?

I hope a crisp, entertaining and enlightening view of what it's like to be in the trenches with a trial lawyer. Hopefully, you'll find it a bit educational as well. But not too heavy in the mechanics of the law.

David. W. Holub

Chapter One

~Solving a Problem~

The sun was coming up on the digital age when I completed law school and passed my bar exams. As an undergrad in the late 1970s, I had concentrated in mathematics and trained in computer programming languages. My senior project was to convert the manual-based college admissions department to a computerized system. Incidentally, that project included an interview with one of the people who helped create part of the programming software that eventually became known as Microsoft Windows NT. The interviewee was at a big-name mainframe company that later sold its intellectual property to Microsoft.

So quite understandably, in my final year of law school, I invested in an IBM PC clone and dot matrix printer. That investment made me one of the first people in my community to own a personal computer. I loved having access to a complete law library on the desk in my home office. Sure, you had to connect to that library using a phone line modem at 1500 baud. But, that slow access rate didn't matter. What mattered was being able to access every legal case, every law encyclopedia, every legal treatise, at any time of day or night from the comfort of my home.

Though I enjoyed the study of mathematics, something you hear few people say, I found the study of law both challenging and refreshing. That is, I enjoyed studying all parts of the law except Constitutional Law. What I discovered about Constitutional Law is that it is not about the study of the Constitution, but in reality, is about the study of what men and women in black robes think about the Constitution and figuring out ways to remember their interpretations and pronouncements about the Constitution. This, I found to be a joyless task.

In my final year of law school, I landed a job as a law clerk for a well-regarded personal injury law firm in Hammond Indiana. This job led to my being hired as an associate a year later. Several years later I became a partner in that firm.

One of my first projects as a young associate was to transition the office from typewriters to desktop PCs. This was a challenge as there were about 15 secretaries who were extremely capable at operating IBM Selectric typing machines, but more than hesitant about switching to computers. Keep in mind that early computer word processing software relied on screen codes and was not a "what you see is what you get" word-processing product. Also, the printers that were available were dot matrix printers and they failed to produce a product that matched the quality of a state-of-the-art typewriter. Nevertheless, the transition to the digital age at my first job went smoothly, as did my transition from law school to trial lawyer.

One of the first projects I worked on with the senior attorney in the firm involved a pour-in-place concrete highway bridge that collapsed during construction. Several workers were killed and others were seriously injured. My role involved investigating what went wrong and included examining the engineering behind the project. I remember flying cross country to examine a room full of 40 boxes of computer printouts, hoping to find a clue as to what went wrong.

After hours of combing through these difficult-to-read computer printouts, I stumbled upon evidence of what had happened. The records suggested that the engineering firm that designed the pour-in-place bridge, had under-designed the concrete pads that were created to hold the scaffolding in place during the concrete pour. The documents suggested that the pads were under-designed by a factor of 10. Essentially, a decimal point data entry mistake is what led to the collapse of the bridge that destroyed a number of lives and disrupted the lives of their family members.

The carelessness made me furious. It was the type of wrong that most every person would want to work to set right. It was at this point in time, as I boarded a plane for home, that I came to see that the law was not a cold subject to be studied and written about, rather it was a tool that I could use along with my talents and training, in courtroom battles to set things right that had gone wrong. I also realized that few lawyers had the problem-solving skills that I had acquired in the study of mathematics and computer science. I began to wonder how I could best combine these skills and talents as I looked to my future as a lawyer.

But, back to the engineering design error that caused so much mayhem. It was breathtaking to consider what had happened. One decimal point error had changed everything for so many people. Children no longer had fathers. Wives became widows in the blink of an eye. Computers were great tools, but were no better than the data entered into them or the humans who operated them.

In short, in this one case I began to see that my mathematics and computer skills, along with my legal training and my curiosity to solve problems, and my desire to try to help set right the lives of those injured as a result of the carelessness of others, could serve as the basis for an impactful legal career.

David W Holub

Chapter Two

~Establishing a Causal Link~

One early case stands out as confirming that my choice to be a trial attorney and work to help set things right for people was the correct one. The client was a young widow with four young children. Her husband had died as result of an automobile crash. But, his death was not linked to the crash in a direct way like you might imagine.

Early one morning while driving on a darkened expressway on the way to work, the young father who was in his mid-30s struck a paving machine mistakenly positioned in the roadway. The machine had no warning lights. There was no flagman. The impact was quite severe, but the young father was thought to have suffered no severe injuries. Still, he was transported to the hospital and checked before being released.

All seemed to be well until while jogging more than a year later he suffered a fatal heart attack. In the interim between the crash and his death, he had seen a cardiologist. He had done so because he felt some occasional chest pain and shortness of breath. But he had passed a stress test and appeared to be just fine.

The challenge for me was, could I establish a causal link between the crash on the expressway and the man's death while jogging? If I could make the link, it would mean a recovery of as much as perhaps $1 million for the man's widow and children. If I could not establish a causal link, it would mean the case would settle for a nominal amount.

The challenge of making a causal connection was complicated by the fact that there was no autopsy. However, upon studying emergency room records, I noted that the deceased had suffered a blow to the chest as the force of the impact rammed the steering wheel against his chest. I also noted that tests run in the emergency room showed an elevation of trace enzymes indicative of a bruise or trauma to the heart.

Another consequence of the dawning of the digital age is that medical articles, like legal case authorities, also became accessible online. I remember spending long hours in the evening using my home computer dialed in at slow modem speeds searching medical journals online for a link between the elevated enzyme readings and the subsequent myocardial infarction.

I would do this research at home while occupied with the normal work of a young associate, mainly legal research and writing, while at the office. This outside the office research was, by my then supervising attorney, considered to be a waste of time. And, back at the dawn of the digital age, you could only access an article index online, you had to contact a repository librarian and purchase copies of the articles and have them mailed.

I was about to give up when, after hours of researching, I finally found several articles linking chest trauma accompanied by high enzyme levels immediately following chest trauma to bruising of the coronary arteries and to myocardial infarction occurring to young individuals within months of such chest trauma. The articles confirmed my suspicion that bruising of the arteries led to abnormal clotting, and the abnormal clotting was linked to causing a heart attack in persons suffering such seemingly non-serious chest injuries.

Let's pause to consider this question. Does the fact that I found online medical support for my theory linking the crash to the heart attack suggest that my supervising attorney should not have been dismissive of my idea? No, not at all. The reality of litigation under the United States legal system is that people who are injured would never be able to pursue a claim against a well-financed insurance carrier or wealthy corporation, if not for attorneys who are willing to work on a contingent fee basis. Meaning that the injured person pays their attorney a portion of the recovery if there is a recovery and pays their attorney nothing if there is no recovery.

Attorney fees range between 33-1/3% up to 50%, on extremely difficult cases. And, though most trial lawyers advance pay the expenses associated with litigation, such as for fees paid to expert consultants, the expenses ultimately are typically paid by the client when the case is concluded.

Short of what I was able to do by searching online on my own time for a causal link between the crash and the heart attack, my firm would have had to locate and pay a top medical doctor at a top university in order to have that medical expert examine the patient's medical records and determine if a causal link existed. This would have cost the client as much as $15,000. If the expert confirmed my theory, the money would've been well spent. But, if the expert rejected my theory, the client's minimal case recovery would have been $15,000 less.

As attorneys we have to always be mindful of the net recovery available to our clients at the end of the case. So, my supervising attorney was 100% correct in his view that it was a waste of money to hire someone to chase my theory. Despite such concerns, I felt the investment of *my time* doing online search in hopes of finding a causal link, as slow and tedious as it was at that point in history, was worth making even if it turned up nothing.

It was extremely rewarding to be able to make a full recovery for the young widow and her children. Perhaps not coincidentally, 20 years later when I opened my own practice, this widow was *the very first person to phone me* on my new office phone line. I had not heard from her in the intervening years. She called simply to thank me and to tell me that her youngest child had just graduated from college and that the money secured in the settlement we obtained linking her husband's death to the car crash had financed college for all of her children.

David W Holub

Chapter Three

~Rising to the Challenge~

The same technology that cost-effectively put an entire law library and an entire medical library at my disposal via a low-speed modem in the early years of my practice in a midsized office of under 40 people, enables me to do today with a staff of under 10 people, more than what law firms of 50 to 100 people used to be able to do before computers. Technology has largely put small and large firms on the same footing.

Gone today, though, are the slow modem speeds that mirrored the slowest of fax machines. For example, today's high-speed internet makes our in-house videoconferencing system a great timesaver and cost saver. No longer can an attorney be pushed to fly to distant venues to depose corporate officers of defendants in products liability cases. Instead, attorneys with state-of-the-art video conferencing equipment like that in our office, can just walk into their conference rooms and turn on the camera and have at it.

I once had a call from a law student who had been given an assignment to ask a small office practitioner what it was like to practice without being with a large number of partners and associates. My response was "I don't know; I don't consider our office to be a small office." The student was speechless. After a moment I explained that I consider my office to be a midsized law firm. I explained that with technology I can do what in the past it took a team of several attorneys to do, and I can do it faster because I know what I'm doing and know how to use the cutting-edge technology at my fingertips. Today, like no other time in history, the size of a law office is largely a mental construct. If you have the technology and you're not intimidated, you can hold your own with, or surpass, the legal brain power of the largest of defense firms.

Since that first personal PC purchase in 1981, I have probably purchased hundreds of PCs, laptops, tablets, smartphones and other high-tech equipment. I am hands-on with technology and have mastered much of the behind-the-scenes technology required to operate networks, network servers, PBX phone systems, and email server systems. If I hadn't decided to focus on being a trial lawyer, I probably would have ended up somewhere in the tech industry. Nevertheless, technology is a tool, but that tool is not equally powerful to all people you have to have the skill, desire and ability to effectively use it.

My knowledge of and experience in technology helped make it an easy decision to open my own office in 2005. Moreover, after I obtained a favorable verdict for my clients in the below-described hard fought trucking case a year earlier, I was confident I could handle the challenges of the courtroom no matter what was thrown at me. Nevertheless, it is a huge advantage that I am blessed with an experienced and enormously dedicated legal team of paralegals, as well as my daughter, who is an attorney and graduate of Indiana University McKinney School of Law.

But back to the point. The case discussed below was a turning point in my professional career, and it is worth spending a few pages discussing it.

The case involved a trucking company that put a dangerous trucker behind the wheel of an 18-wheeler. He rear-ended my client and tore her car in half. At issue was a serious injury to my client, but also conduct that to me bordered on criminal recklessness on the part of the trucking company. The jury must have agreed with my assessment as to the conduct of the trucking company, because the verdict included a component for punitive damages.

At first glance the trucking company seemed to have fully complied with Federal Motor Carrier regulations. These regulations require motor carriers to periodically evaluate drivers and take them off the road if they exceed the maximum number of moving violations within a set period of time. Well, the driver of this truck at the time of the crash had lots of moving violations, and to my thinking should have been disqualified to drive, yet the company found him to be fit and qualified to drive.

However, what I found upon analyzing the records of the motor carrier was that instead of reviewing the driver on a set timetable as called for by the letter of the regulations, the carrier was not looking at a fixed time period when it reviewed its drivers. Instead, the company would immediately evaluate a driver whenever the driver would get a second moving violation. Then, when the third or fourth moving violation inevitably would come in, the company would again evaluate the driver, but the carrier *would ignore any violations that occurred before the last evaluation* of the driver.

Thus, the carrier had defeated the spirit, if not the letter, of the law requiring periodic review of operator driving records. In doing so, it trumpeted the fact that it was reviewing drivers *more often than required* and was thus, to its way of thinking, being *extra* safe. But, the jury understood it was all a scam.

The scam being run to keep bad drivers on the road was very inventive, and not easy to discern. I am not sure how many other trial lawyers would've taken the time to plod through the records to uncover what was going on. It takes time and work, and doggedness, to uncover what happens often behind the scenes of a negligence case. It would have been easy to have not undertaken this extra work, and instead said "this is a rear end collision and clearly the driver is at fault, so what is served by investigating further?"

For some reason, however, I was furious at what had happened to my client (and could have happened to anyone sharing the highway with this particular trucker), and I would not stop until I sorted out why the driver was behind the wheel and why the carrier went to such lengths to keep him behind the wheel. I further uncovered that he was related to an owner of one of the companies involved in the crash, which likely influenced the decision to keep him behind the wheel. That fury or anger led to extra effort on my part to uncover what had happened and present all the facts to the jury. Those uncovered facts likely were a major reason why the verdict was as large as it was and why the jury awarded punitive damages at a multiple of fifteen times the amount of compensatory damages.

The favorable verdict was obtained in a fight against a large Chicago law firm experienced in defending trucking companies. The verdict made me realize that a good trial result is not dependent on the number of attorneys sitting at counsel table, but rather depends on a trial lawyer working hard to find the truth and presenting that truth to a jury. Surely too, the verdict depended in the greatest part on a jury made up of caring citizens who, like me, were furious with the conduct of a trucking company with driver qualification review practices of the nature disclosed by the evidence.

That verdict was meant by the jury to send a message to trucking companies tempted to conduct themselves in similar reckless and wanton ways. Juries play a critically important role in our system of justice. The Seventh Amendment in the Bill of Rights to the Constitution reads:

"In Suits at common law, where the value in controversy shall exceed twenty dollars, the right to trial by jury shall be preserved, and no fact tried by a jury, shall be otherwise re-examined in any Court of the United States, than according to the rules of the common law."

In this language, the Constitution makes crystal clear that citizen judges stand in protection of our freedom. In nations where tyranny rules, tyranny is enforced by a judicial system of professional legal experts who control every aspect of community life. The right of citizens to speak as the conscience of the community is as important to staving off tyranny, as is the right to speak your mind freely, to choose your religion, to not be unreasonably searched, to bear arms in self-defense, in short, as important as every other protection contained in the Bill of Rights.

Every citizen who has answered the call to serve as a juror deserves a salute. Any one of us may at any time end up as a victim of the reckless conduct of others. I think my fellow citizens deciding the case realized this. My client just happened to be in the wrong place at the wrong time. The facts uncovered at trial made clear that the defendant driver who upended the life of our client should never have been on the road that day and, had regulations been properly followed, he should've been benched and on the sidelines at the time of the crash.

David W Holub

Chapter Four

~Life is Fragile~

Near the end of 2005, I opened my own office. At that point in time, coming off of the $16.1 million verdict obtained the year before in the above-described trucking case, I was tabulated by an independent verdict tabulating organization to have had the highest dollar verdict obtained in the State of Indiana for clients as of 2004.

The Indiana Jury Verdict Reporter, at http://www.juryverdicts.net completed this tabulation. In so noting, the publisher also noted that the chance of getting a million-dollar verdict in an auto negligence case that year was less than 1%, based on 194 auto collision cases tried to Indiana juries in 2004. What is the takeaway? It means that it is *impossible* to look at an outcome in one case and predict future success or think that an attorney can achieve the same results in another future case, and anyone reading this book is *not to draw* any other conclusion.[1]

---

[1] Here is general advice for those considering hiring an attorney touting a high verdict in an ad. Ask them to explain: a) if the verdict is reduced for comparative or non-party fault (defendants don't pay for conduct caused by a non-party or the plaintiff); b) if the recovery is capped (there are caps on government liability and medical malpractice cases); c) if the defendant has resources or insurance to pay the

The results my clients obtained in that trucking case gave me cause for concern, however, as to what the future held for me as a trial lawyer and how, in general, things would go as I opened my own office. Would the verdict be sustained on appeal? Would a different jury have decided differently? We know as lawyers that when cases have to be retried to a different jury, different results sometimes occur.

Sometimes trial lawyers wait their entire lifetime for an important and interesting case, and I feared that I had already been allocated by fate my most interesting case. Despite being a bit apprehensive, and having no answers to these questions, I proceeded to open my own law office. But my fear of not having another challenging case proved wrong.

With no fanfare whatsoever, I met with a young mother and father who came to see me about their son, a young boy who had contracted the vaccinia virus when his father, a soldier set to be deployed to Iraq, had been vaccinated for smallpox contrary to medical screening requirements.

---

verdict; d) if the verdict can be reduced by a trial judge or on appeal; and, e) if the verdict is payable to the government as is the case with punitive damages.

The vaccinia virus is something doctors would see frequently in the 1950s when people were routinely vaccinated for smallpox but, since the eradication of smallpox, no physician in approximately 25 years had encountered a patient with the vaccinia virus.

The boy contracted the vaccinia virus from his father, who had been vaccinated before being deployed to a war zone. This was eventually deduced by top physicians at Rush University Medical Center in Chicago, but the illness had progressed to an alarming point before the diagnosis was made. Imagine a victim of smallpox, one of the worst and deadliest diseases known, with 80% of their body covered with all-encompassing rashes and boils, and you'll get a good picture of what happened to this young boy.

The PBS News Hour show picked up the story. A 15-minute segment of the show (carefully preserving family anonymity) in audio and video format was still accessible online at my last check, indexed under the search term "vaccinia virus". The program describes how the boy was hospitalized in isolation and in intensive care for weeks in a medically induced coma. The show details how the smallpox vaccine is a "live virus" administered to encourage the body to develop immunity to smallpox.

Candidates must be carefully screened before a medical decision is made to give the vaccine.

The vaccination was given despite a medical screening that determined two clear and well-recognized contraindications: a) the serviceman had a prior medical history of a skin ailment known as eczema or atopic dermatitis, and b) members of the serviceman's household (and in particular the young boy) at the time of the vaccination had a history of suffering with eczema.

Doctors were of course baffled by the appearance of a disease not encountered for years, and initially were concerned that the boy was the victim of a terror attack. Family members were initially quarantined until the medical team treating the boy figured out what was wrong with him.

We were very thankful that we were able to obtain compensation for what happened to the boy, who made a full medical recovery. Working on such cases reminds me just how fragile life is, and how we all depend on each other to get through life.

Initially, the medical records of the soldier, which we needed to prove that he had been improperly vaccinated, were reported as "missing". Perhaps someone involved in giving him the vaccine was trying to protect his or her job. Nevertheless, we eventually were able to track down the key medical records, which included a questionnaire which was properly completed by the soldier and red flagged him as someone who should NOT get the vaccine. The medical doctor who authorized the vaccination had initially testified that there were no contraindications for administering the vaccine. But the records, once found, proved otherwise.

A young soldier was prepared to give his life for his country if need be, and his young son's life was put at risk, all because giving the father the vaccine was contraindicated, precisely because giving it to him would make him contagious and at risk to pass on the virus, not just to his son, but to anyone he might encounter.

But, though a mistake was made in vaccinating the father, I was in awe of the doctors who pulled out all the stops to save the boy, and of the willingness of the government to let the doctors try untested medications on the boy (when conventional treatments proved to be ineffective), which eventually reversed the course of the disease. When we work together as a people, the people of the USA are amazing.

David W Holub

Chapter Five

~Unreasonably Dangerous~

I am not sure what it is with me and small children, but this next case involved the death of a toddler when a large cathode-ray TV was accidentally tipped over by his young brother and sister and crushed the toddler. Like the vaccinia virus case, this case cried out to me, and thankfully we were able to make a recovery for the family, all of whom were understandably devastated by the loss of the young child.

Here is what happened. A four-year-old and eight-year-old were playing in their bedroom in front of an old family television that had been put on top of the kids' dresser. Their brother was crawling around on the floor in front of the TV. The four-year-old sister playfully tried to block her older brother's view of the television screen, and the older brother lifted his sister's ankles up off the floor to his chest height so he could pull her away from the television. In an effort to continue blocking the screen, she held tightly onto the top of the television while her brother, began tugging on his sister's ankles. After the third tug, the television she had been grabbing onto tipped forward off the dresser and landed on their brother. Hearing a loud sound, the mother rushed into the room to find her child crushed under the weight of the fallen television.

Though at the time we took this case the law was against us, and it was unlikely that we would prevail, our entire litigation team felt that the case simply had to be pursued. We argued that the television manufacturer's product was unreasonably dangerous and unfit for its intended purposes. While the case ultimately was resolved via a confidential settlement, it was the first reported television tip-over case in the country to survive a summary judgment motion. This is the type of motion which judges usually decide against a plaintiff and use to dismiss a case and toss the claim out of court.

Unfortunately, as we soon learned, television and furniture tip-over incidents occur all too often. At a time in which people are purchasing large flat screen televisions for their living rooms, older televisions often are relocated to bedrooms, including children's rooms, where they are commonly placed on top of a dresser. Many parents are unaware of the danger of television and furniture tip-overs.

Parents do not get a handout when their baby is brought home from the hospital warning them to anchor the television or other furniture to the wall with brackets and straps to prevent these pieces of furniture from tipping over and falling onto children and injuring them. On the other hand, new parents are often warned of the dangers posed by electrical outlets, or cupboards containing medications, solvents, and cleaning supplies. Consequently, few parents recognize the danger presented by televisions.

In many instances, it only takes a minimal amount of force applied to the top of the television to cause the tip-over. What often happens is, in an attempt to reach the television controls, a child pulls out and stands on dresser drawers or otherwise climbs, reaches, or grabs at the television, which causes the television to tip-over onto the child. The types of injuries that can occur from tip-overs include skull fractures, crush injuries, and death.

One difficulty in bringing a claim against a manufacturer of an older television is that the product may be near the ten-year statute of repose limit (if a product is older than ten years fails, the maker generally cannot be sued) or the manufacturer may be out of business. Manufacturers that are out of business may not have insurance to cover claims. Also, it is nearly impossible to collect money from a company that has long been out of business. In our case, the manufacturer was out of business when the complaint was filed, but there *was* an insurance policy covering the television.

The next challenge was finding corporate records for a defunct manufacturer. Additionally, it became crucial for us to do thorough research of medical and other academic journal articles about the type of product in question to see if its dangers had been documented in any published literature. Fortunately, we were able to find several medical journal articles by emergency department physicians who had treated dying children, who had been crushed in a television tip-over incident. The physician-authors warned about the dangers of television tip-over injuries and implored manufacturers to make safer products.

When we were reading the medical journal articles, we also learned that the Product Safety Working Group committee of the Consumer Electronics Association (CEA) had been approached by several of the article authors who wanted the televisions to be designed more safely or have stringent warnings affixed. We did a non-party request to obtain all of the minutes from the CEA's Product Safety Working Group committee. These records were extremely helpful.

Armed with medical journal articles, we were able to pin down a former high-level engineer for the manufacturer during a deposition and establish that the manufacturer had participated in the meetings of the CEA's Product Safety Working Group Committee. The engineer acknowledged that the type of tip-over dangers described in the medical journal articles were discussed in the safety group meetings. Also, he testified that, in general, the dangers noted in each of the medical journal articles were known to engineers in charge of the design and safety of the televisions well before they were sold.

Using the information gained in the deposition of the engineer for the manufacturer, we were able to successfully argue for the plaintiffs that the manufacturer sold the television in an unsafe condition, knowing it was unsafe, and nevertheless represented that the television was safe. The manufacturer had inadequately warned of the risks of the tip-overs and otherwise failed to disclose information about the proper use of the television, both of which arguably amounted to a design defect. Key evidence in our case showed that the manufacturer actually considered a retro-fit program and a post-sale warning campaign on the dangers of tip-overs, but did not take steps to implement either program, nor did it take steps to recall the product.

Helping this family was important to our team. Equally important, though was setting a legal precedent that hopefully will encourage manufacturers to set child safety as a top priority so that *other children may be saved.*

Chapter Six

~Anatomy of a Rescue~

Aside from the cases mentioned in earlier chapters, and it is a great honor to assist families who have lost a child or who are struggling with bills mounting up to treat a gravely ill child, I have also had the privilege of representing several "rescuers" as the law describes them.

Rescuers are heroes and as I will explain, the law recognizes them as such. However, advocating on behalf of a hero has its own special challenges - not the least of which is to remember that no rescue is complete until the jury returns a verdict setting right what happened to your client.

In one case a man saved a co-worker from electrocution by knocking him loose from energized power lines with which the co-worker had become entangled. Another case involved the estate of a trucker who died trying to rescue people in a fast flooding subdivision by building an emergency levee when he raised the bed of his truck into a high-power line. In still another case, a customer saved a store cashier's life during an armed robbery by wrestling the robber to the ground and was shot during the encounter (other customers ran and hid). The common thread: each rescue injury victim acted at grave risk to themselves to try to save others.

I could devote a chapter to each hero noted above but discussing the individual who intervened during an armed robbery I believe will best illustrate the challenges posed by such cases. Accordingly, what follows describes what happened in that case.

At approximately 6:00 p.m. on a cold January evening, our client was injured during a store robbery while he was a business invitee and customer at the store. The store premises had before the robbery experienced criminal activity for years (including a prior strong-arm robbery). Nevertheless, the store owner did not have an on premises security guard, nor did it maintain adequate security equipment to control and deter criminal activity, and it failed to conduct a badly needed criminal security survey which would have exposed the dangers plaguing the store.

The rescue by our client, and the shooting of our client, was captured on surveillance video. During the robbery there was an announcement over the store intercom system by a female cashier. She sounded stressed and panicked. Then the announcement ended abruptly. Our client rightly concluded that the cashier was in peril. The cashier who was being robbed in fact called out to our client for help. She appears on the video of the robbery struggling with the robber until our client responds to her call for help. Then the video shows the hooded robber struggle with our client, shoot him, and then flee.

Clearly our client engaged in a "rescue", but what exactly is the "rescue doctrine". In short, the rescue doctrine grants leeway to spontaneous voluntary selfless acts undertaken to save human life or property. In other words, the rescue doctrine permits one who has negligently endangered the safety of another (or himself) to be held liable under the law for any injuries sustained by a person who is hurt attempting a rescue.

The essence of the rescue doctrine is that the law allows a person injured while attempting to rescue someone from danger, where the rescue requires immediate and rapid action without time for deliberation, to assume extraordinary risks and to perform acts which might be considered negligent in other circumstances, provided that the rescuer's conduct does not amount to recklessness.

Essentially, the rescue doctrine provides that it is always foreseeable that someone may attempt to rescue a person who has been placed in a dangerous position and that the rescuer may incur injuries in doing so, and thus, if a defendant has acted negligently toward the person being rescued, he has acted negligently toward the rescuer.

In the case involving the shooting of our client during a robbery, we gathered additional evidence, through depositions of employees, and by obtaining and analyzing years of police reports of crime in the neighborhood and established that a robbery at the store was foreseeable (given prior incidents, escalating crime on the premises, unheeded requests for more security by employees, and a conscious disregard of the crime history and statistics for the location).

In fact, the crime related information known at the time of the shooting, included:
- An increase in shopliftings;
- An increase in the value of the merchandise being taken;
- An increase in the "boldness" of the shoplifters- taking large items including electric fans;
- An increase in the frequency of shoplifter/employee confrontations;

- The prior employment of security guards at an "old store" operated by the same owner across the street;
- The use of security guards and police officers to provide security at a nearby grocery store and gas station;
- And a prior strong-arm robbery at the very store where our client was shot.

We successfully argued that considering these factors the likelihood of violence occurring inside this store, either by shoplifters or armed or unarmed robbers of cashiers was known or should have been known. Further, our evidence showed that a reasonably trained and competent security manager would have concluded that additional security measures were required to protect merchandise, employees, and patrons.

At the time of the violent assault with a firearm against our client, no security measures were in place at the store, other than cameras. The evidence we put together also established that had a security survey been conducted, the most reasonable and cost-effective conclusion to be drawn from a survey would have been to place uniformed security officers in the store to patrol the interior of the store and maintain a frequent presence at the cashier area where the guard could be observed by patrons and potential lawbreakers to provide a visible deterrent.

The rescue doctrine encompasses those situations where someone has been put at risk of injury as a result of the negligence of another. The doctrine provides that "one who has, through his negligence, endangered the safety of another may be held liable for the injuries sustained by a third person in attempting to save such other from injury." In applying the rescue doctrine, "wisdom of hindsight is not determinative on the issue of the doctrine's applicability. So long as the rescue attempted can be said to have been a reasonable course of conduct at the time, it is of no import that the danger was not as real as it appeared."

But, in representing our clients in rescue cases, we have to deal with the fact that potential jurors may in fact try to analyze our client's conduct through the prism of hindsight. People react very differently when confronted with a rescue scenario. Keep in mind, though our client was injured when he saved the store cashier's life during an armed robbery by wrestling the robber to the ground, a dozen other customers in the store ran and hid during the robbery; each was prepared to testify that the plaintiff *should also have hidden* and should not have risked getting involved. Knowing in advance how jurors might react to such testimony is critical to effectively presenting a case.

People who are afraid to risk themselves to save another person will *always* be able to justify their attitude and actions in their own minds. For example, a person might think "I would have had to run and hide, my kids wouldn't survive if I were killed." It is important to anticipate how such people might impact deliberations. Will they argue that the plaintiff was reckless for getting involved? Will they argue that the plaintiff should have waited for a professional rescuer to arrive? Will there be someone on the jury to argue on behalf of the person who took a risk? Will the risk that was taken be viewed as reasonable and justified? Will the people asked to serve on the jury run from the hard questions posed by the fact of the rescue, or will they stand up for justice and help set things right for the rescuer who was injured?

As noted earlier, it is always an honor to represent a rescuer or the family of a rescuer, but there are unique challenges to face when you undertake to do so.

David W Holub

Chapter Seven

~The Case of Miss M. ~

Of the many types of cases we deal with as trial lawyers, one of the most challenging of cases is the medical malpractice case. The challenges stem from many reasons, but the major reason is that medical treatment information is complex and difficult to understand. Plus, to prove your case you must rely on the testimony of medical doctors. Imagine if you were suing a baseball player for hitting a ball through your window and breaking it. Then imagine that all the witnesses in the case, on the issue of whether the baseball player was careless, are other baseball players. Putting together evidence to persuade a jury in such a situation would be difficult, wouldn't it?

This book would not be complete, however, without a chapter discussing medical malpractice. The case noted in this chapter is fairly representative of what is encountered in representing a family that has been the victim of malpractice. This case resulted in a verdict for the family, but many malpractice cases result in a verdict for the doctor or hospital, no matter how hard fought the battle.

This case involved Miss M., a 55-year-old woman with chronic obstructive pulmonary disease (COPD) who was brought to the emergency room of the defendant hospital because she was having difficulty breathing. In the emergency room, Miss M. was urgently intubated (meaning that a breathing tube was inserted in her mouth and throat) and she was placed on a ventilator. At the time of her arrival at the hospital, she had approximately 50% of normal lung function. After several days in the ICU for treatment of her lungs and a mild heart attack, Miss M. improved and the breathing tube was removed.

If the story ended at this point, Miss M. should have been released to go home to her family. But, the story does not end here. Instead of heading home to her family, Miss M. died 23 days after she placed herself into the hospital's care.

The question was why? What happened to her? The first clue came about 6 days after Miss M. was admitted to the hospital. At this 6-day mark, she was noted to have blood in her mouth. But, astonishingly, the bleeding was not investigated until 10 days after being admitted to the hospital.

The hospital made a simple but fatal mistake. The hospital failed to locate and remove Miss M.'s partial dentures when she arrived at the hospital in a semi-conscious state. The troubling details of how this led to her death follow.

Importantly, in many malpractice cases the mistakes that result in injury or death are very simple mistakes. For example, the task of checking an unconscious or semi-conscious person's mouth for dentures is simple, but the ramifications of not checking can be fatal, as it was in this case.

What the evidence showed is that Miss M.'s partial dentures were never located and accounted for when she arrived at the hospital. Instead, the evidence showed that the partial dentures loosened and dropped down into Miss M.'s throat after the breathing tube was removed. This explains why Miss M. initially improved after being admitted to the ICU. The partial likely stayed in place when the breathing tube was placed but dislodged when the breathing tube was removed. Because dentures were not properly accounted for when the breathing tube was first inserted, hospital employees did not suspect that the partial dentures dropped down Miss M.'s throat when the tubing was removed.

That the dentures must have dropped down Miss M.'s throat at the removal of the breathing tube was further borne out by nursing chart entries. Shortly after Miss M.'s extubation (tube removal), a nurse noted bleeding in Miss M.'s mouth, but was not concerned and did not investigate it, or call a doctor to investigate it. The hospital's position was that there should be no concern about a foreign object – partial dentures – when the expectation at tube removal was that any possible foreign object danger was dealt with when the tube was inserted.

What happened next should have set off an alarm. Miss M. was taken to have a routine MRI. After she returned from the MRI, a nurse noted that blood was running out of Miss M.'s mouth and pooling on her bed pillow and that her blood pressure was low. By this time the partial dentures had more than likely become lodged in her throat, cutting her throat and causing her to bleed internally. At this point the metal in the partial dentures was probably pressed into Miss M.'s throat by the magnetic pull of the MRI machine.

Still not concerned, the nurse simply tried to raise Miss M.'s blood pressure by raising the foot of her bed to place Miss M.'s head lower than her feet in what is called the Trendelenburg position. Not knowing of the dentures cutting into Miss M.'s throat, the nurse unwittingly made the blood channel into Miss M.'s lungs, by setting her head lower than her feet, causing her to develop aspiration pneumonia which ultimately led to her death. This, I argued on closing, was the equivalent of waterboarding Miss M. in her own blood.

It took 10 days after Miss M. was admitted (4 days after the bleeding started) for the dentures to be discovered and removed. By the time the dentures were discovered, Miss M. had already experienced many hours of bleeding in her throat where the dentures had cut her. Because of the bleeding, she needed to be intubated again. She required the infusion of nearly two liters of blood and fluids to regain blood pressure after going into hypovolemic shock caused by inadequate blood volume. Because her blood pressure dropped precipitously, her already difficult-to-find veins collapsed.

So, in order to infuse her with IV fluids, a catheter was urgently placed in her jugular. The needle used to do this punctured her lung causing a collapsed lung. She then functioned with 25% lung capacity while on a ventilator, and pneumonia developed in her lungs. She died not long after that.

Before the dentures dropped down into Miss M.'s throat and cut her, Miss M.'s health had been improving steadily in the ICU. Our expert testified that she had a 60% chance of leaving the hospital and living for two years had the bleeding incident not occurred.

A seven-member jury returned a verdict against the hospital and awarded a substantial sum to the family despite a vigorous defense. The defense argued that the bleeding from the mouth was not significant and that Miss M. *died simply because she wore out*. To the multiple defense expert physicians, the bleeding was a minor complication of no consequence.

This lawsuit succeeded even in the face of a pre-suit medical review panel's favorable finding for the hospital. Before a malpractice case can go to trial in Indiana it has to go before a medical review panel of three doctors. The three doctors who reviewed this case before trial all agreed that the hospital was *blameless*, and the law requires that the jury be informed that a review panel had exonerated the hospital.

As I hope this case study makes clear, medical malpractice cases are extremely difficult. The analogy of suing a baseball player where all the witnesses are on the side of the baseball player, is quite accurate. Winning cases like these are rewarding, however. After trial Miss M.'s sister wrote me the following note, which I have carefully preserved: *"I appreciate your ability to see the merit in pursuing the suit, when other lawyers gave us so little hope or encouragement. Thank you ..."*

David W Holub

Chapter Eight

~Reasonable Care~

A noteworthy part of my practice has involved class action litigation. In class actions, one or two plaintiffs represent a group of people, called a class, who have similar claims. For simplicity, the court permits several individuals to be "class representatives", and they proceed to trial as a "test case" and the result of that test case sets the stage for resolving the individual claims of the entire class.

My longest class action trial lasted nine weeks. I have been involved in a number of class actions either as lead counsel or co-lead counsel for the class representatives named in the lawsuits. One case involved a group of college students cheated by their college, another case involved property owners surrounding a hazardous waste landfill, still another case involved 375 families in a subdivision that was flooded during a rainstorm, not because it rained more than expected, but because the defendants in that case tore down a protective levee by mistake and failed to reconstruct it to the proper height when ordered by the government to rebuild it.

As you might imagine, it is an enormous challenge to undertake to help repair the lives of 375 families all at once. Just think for a moment about the harms these families suffered. Their homes and furnishings and other personal property were destroyed. But, they also suffered injury and damage to their persons including an affront to their bodies and psyches. They also suffered a permanent diminution of market value of their real property, temporary loss of use or rental value of their property, and loss of value of improvements, fixtures, trees, crops, etc. Moreover, there were incidental expenses, as well as inconvenience, discomfort, and annoyance.

But as I hinted a moment ago, this was not a naturally caused flood, but a flood caused by carelessness by governmental officials, careless engineers, and contractors. Let me explain by way of this illustration. Fill your kitchen sink with water and then take an ordinary cereal bowl and slowly push it into the water until the rim is just a hair's width above the waterline. Now imagine that the rim of the bowl is a levee, a barrier preventing the water from entering the bowl. Now imagine that inside of the bowl is a subdivision containing 375 families.

If you were to cut a groove anywhere around the rim of the bowl, the bowl would immediately fill with water. The larger the groove the quicker the water would flood in and overwhelm the 375 families in the bowl. This is in a nutshell what happened to those 375 families.

Here is what happened in greater detail. The facts we were able to piece together established that the damage to the subdivision was brought about by the defendants' failed attempt to properly reconstruct a degraded railroad embankment that for years had functioned as a levee, protecting the subdivision from the waters of a nearby river. The railroad embankment that was degraded was adjacent to a business parking lot. Months before the subdivision was deluged, the defendants (engineers, governmental agencies, and contractors) ascertained that the levee had been degraded during a parking lot expansion project initiated on the parcel near the embankment.

The governmental defendants collectively agreed to, and undertook to, reconstruct the levee via a half-hearted effort to compel the parking lot excavation contractors and engineers to rebuild the levee. The contractor and engineering defendants' efforts to see that the levee was satisfactorily reconstructed failed, as did the governmental defendants' joint efforts to direct, supervise, and approve their work.

Put again in the terms of our bowl and kitchen sink analogy, contractors cut into the rim around the bowl that protected the subdivision from being flooded. The government found out about the cut and ordered the cut in the rim repaired. Repairs were made, and the government signed off on the repairs, but the rim was not repaired correctly. Yet the government signed off on the repairs without confirming that the repairs were properly made.

The plaintiff class representatives' main argument was that the governmental and private defendants failed to use reasonable care in the reconstruction of the levee, once undertaking the obligation to see that it was reconstructed. Thereby, the defendants contributed to the creation and maintenance of a nuisance.

For many years before the flood, the subdivision was protected from overflow waters of the river by the railroad line embankment along the western border of the subdivision, which had been established around the year 1900. The embankment ran along the entire western border of the parcel where the parking lot was expanded, separating the property from a golf course to the west. Before its destruction, whenever the river overflowed its banks, the excess waters would flow onto the adjacent golf course to the west and were blocked by the railroad embankment so that they posed no threat to the subdivision.

When the railroads were constructed, they were built at a consistent elevation and when tied in with other structures would provide a reliable first line of protection against floods. The railroad embankment was constructed at 600-feet United States Government Survey (USGS). This elevation provided 1-foot freeboard above the estimated 100-year flood stage of 599-feet USGS. Long before this incident, the US Army Corps of Engineers incorporated the railroad embankment into a plan for a comprehensive flood control system of levees which included protection for the subdivision.

The failed reconstruction efforts of the defendants were traced directly to the reconstructed embankment where the water had entered not being up to the required 600 feet USGS level, but rather it was several feet too low and was not capable of providing the expected and reliable flood protection. The flooding event reached an elevation of approximately 598.4 feet to 598.6 feet USGS at the site. Consequently, the evidence was clear that if there had been a reconstruction of the embankment at 600' USGS, the flood would not have occurred.

Because we were able to establish clear evidence of wrongdoing, although we battled with the defendants over which ones were most at fault and whether the governmental entities involved were entitled to immunity, we were able to obtain a settlement fund for the 375 families hurt by the carelessness of the defendants. However, obtaining a settlement fund was not the hard part. The difficult part was coming up with a fair way to distribute the fund to the 375 families. This is where mathematics again came to the rescue.

News regarding social media and targeted advertising often uses the word "algorithm". The word describes a defined set of rules, or formula, to be followed in making calculations or solving a problem.

In order to distribute the settlement fund, I came up with a formula to apply to all the data we collected about the 375 families harmed by the flood. Without running off into the weeds about the details of the algorithm, it took into account things like square footage of each home that was destroyed, the number of occupants in a home, whether the occupants were owners or renters, the estimated dollar value of cars and furniture and other items of personal property lost, etc.

The distribution formula was well-received by the 375 families, and when we sought court approval for it not one objection was raised. We used an ordinary computer-based spreadsheet to apply the formula and tabulate the distribution of settlement proceeds to the penny.

I remember working over Thanksgiving weekend to run and then rerun the calculations to make certain that everything was perfect. Then I printed off and signed all the checks going out to the 375 families. We got them in the mail to everyone well before Christmas. Signing those checks for the 375 families was one of the most enjoyable tasks I have ever had the pleasure to complete as a trial lawyer.

David W Holub

Chapter Nine

~Uncovering Nefarious Activity~

This may come as no surprise to some readers but, when it comes to litigation, far too many people lie. People sometimes will claim they had a green light when in fact their light was red. Corporations and their officers and employees will lie to get out of paying money or to save their jobs. And, sometimes in addition to lying, people will fabricate evidence. But, though it is also true that many people are honorable and tell the truth (thank goodness, because justice depends on it) the case noted below highlights how perseverance and taking nothing at face value is often needed to uncover the truth, especially when the lies are elaborate.

The following railroad crossing case illustrates how even event recorder data must be carefully analyzed for potential manipulation. The rule of law as to when a train traversing a rail crossing has the right-of-way is simple. At an unprotected crossing with no flashers or gates, the train must sound its whistle in order to claim the right-of-way. The whistle is a warning to traffic that the train is near and that the train is claiming the right-of-way to cross the roadway. This rule has been around since the development of railroads.

But rarely when there is a train and car crash involving an unprotected railroad crossing will the locomotive engineer or conductor say anything other than "yes, of course we blew the whistle appropriately as we approached the crossing." Moreover, locomotive engineers remarkably seem to always blow the whistle long and hard right after impact with a car or truck. This produces a number of ear witnesses who say "sure I heard a whistle."

Unfortunately, the driver of the car or truck that collided with the train is usually not around to be a witness since trains frequently come out the winner in such crashes. So, if the train operators decline to be truthful, is there a way to prove what really happened when the case looks hopeless and the readily available evidence points to the car failing to yield the right of way to the train? Sometimes there is.

Each rail locomotive is equipped with an event recorder. This event recorder records speed, brake application, and whether the horn (what we call a whistle) has been sounded. So, if you obtain the event recorder data, you can confirm what really happened, right? Maybe.

There is a very important variable in respect to locomotive event recorder data that can be manipulated by a company bent on hiding what really happened. Have you guessed what it is? It is the position of the train on the tracks. You might have event recorder data that shows the sounding of a horn, but where on the tracks did that horn sound? Before the crossing? At the time the train was at the crossing? After the crossing?

In "railroad speak" a train made up of a locomotive engine and railcars is called a "consist". When a train leaves the station, precise mile marker information is entered into the event recorder. Indiana is roughly 140 miles wide. Since rails must be meticulously maintained, every inch of track is well known to and tracked by railroad operators. A railroad company with track running the width of the state, for example, will know exactly where the head and tail of each consist is located as it moves across the state when an accurate starting point is entered into the event recorder at the beginning of the journey. If a crossing crash happens at, say, the 80.91-mile point, and if the first sounding of a horn is right at the 80.91-mile point of the event recorder, the railroad has a big problem.

A horn is supposed to be sounded in a special sequence of long and short blasts beginning at least a quarter mile before the crossing. But all a skilled technician needs to do to make a lie look like the truth is to change the starting point of the consist when downloading and analyzing the data. Not every company equips locomotives with GPS tags, which help to frustrate the manipulation of recorder data.

How does one go about uncovering such nefarious activity? To answer that question, we need to discuss what event recorder data looks like. For information like whether the horn or brakes are activated at any given time, the data is simply the numbers one or zero. Such data is usually noted every second. For every second of operation the horn is either on or off. The brakes are either on or off.

If a horn is actually sounded a quarter-mile from a crossing, the brakes should be off. Why would a competent engineer apply brakes for no purpose a quarter-mile before a crossing? But if the crash has just occurred and the engineer sounds a horn and applies the brakes at the same time, and there are no other horns being sounded within a half-mile before the crash point, such information strongly suggests no horn was used to claim the right of way before the crash.

Since a starting point of a consist can be manipulated after a crash, by entering a *different* starting point at the time the data is downloaded, what if a railroad company implements an unspoken policy to not brake at impact or sound a horn at impact, in a situation where a crash occurs due to a failure to sound a horn as required by law? What if the railroad instead waits and sounds a horn about a quarter-mile after impact, and then start braking another quarter-mile after that? This creates a horn sound for ear witnesses to hear, but allows for the manipulation of event recorder data by altering the location of the consist in order to paint a picture of compliance with the law. Keep in mind this likely would not work for a passenger train where passengers would hear the crash and see the aftermath. But for a 100 railcar consist with just an engineer and conductor on board, and no photos showing where the train stopped in relation to the crossing, there may be a temptation to manipulate the data.

If someone is this devious and waits to sound a horn until well after the impact, is there a way to catch them in the deception? Well in one case a way was found to unravel such deceit.

In that case, the consist was made up of two locomotives and about 100 railcars. After the crash, event recorder data was secured, as the law requires, from the lead engine. After examining the data there was a concern as to its validity, so the event recorder data from the other engine was obtained and was downloaded by a different technician, who downloaded the default location data without modification. In this particular case, before the request for the data from the second engine, the only data that was secured by the railroad company came from the lead locomotive.

When two engines are part of a consist, one is enslaved to the other, meaning the engineer in the master locomotive engine can control both engines through the controls of the master engine. But even though one engine is enslaved to the other, their event recorders remain separate and record independently what happens as experienced by each locomotive engine. Thank goodness event recorders can't be turned off or disabled.

When the event recorder data from the slave engine was obtained, it showed a different starting point on the track. The difference was just enough to make it more likely than not that the horn was not sounded a quarter mile before the crossing as the law requires. The manipulation of event recorder data at download does not take rocket scientist skills, all you need to do is know what the real starting point of the consist is (which appears when you begin the data download) and then adjust the distance by a half mile (or whatever distance you need) because you know where the front of the engine stopped after impact.

The second engine data provided persuasive evidence that the data for the master engine had perhaps been manipulated after the crash to hide the fact that no horn was blown before impact at the crossing. Or, at the very least, it illustrated that the railroad was sloppy and entered erroneous starting point data into the data retrieved from at least one of the two engine recorders. Obtaining this evidence was important to set the stage for the case to be concluded by way of a fair settlement.

What trial lawyers do is not as exciting as what you see on the investigation TV shows like NCIS. But, experienced trial lawyers across the nation, especially those who have a dedicated team of professionals like we do, work in much the same fashion, consulting experts where needed, when it comes to working to discern the truth in the midst of an effort to hide it.

A former partner of mine once said that I was the most aggressive attorney he knew. I decided to take that as a compliment, though that may not have been intended. What I do know is that at our office we battle hard to get to the truth for clients. A dog intently chewing on a bone is the image that comes to mind. It also means that we need and require our clients to be absolutely truthful with us. We rarely hesitate to aggressively expend energy, time, and money to prove that our client is in the right when we believe in the cause of our client.

Chapter Ten
~A Wild Ride~

The TV tip-over case mentioned earlier is a typical product liability case. The case below is a bit of a hybrid. It involves a machine, amusement ride equipment to be precise, that was safe if operated according to the owner's manual supplied by the manufacturer, but in this case, the operation of the equipment was anything but safe.

More particularly, our client was a patron of a traveling carnival show at a county fair when she boarded a ride designed to simulate weightlessness experienced in a spaceship. The "spaceship ride" is a ride where the rider is spun in a circular motion on the inside wall of a large conical cylinder. Throughout the ride, the rider is standing on a sled-like panel, which is against an angled wall on the interior of the cylinder. Once the ride is spinning fast enough, the rider slides up the angled wall on the sled toward the top edge of the cylinder.

While our client was riding the "spaceship ride", the ride operator repetitively changed the ride speed from higher to lower then to higher again, which caused the passenger panel on which she was leaning, to move up and down violently as the force on the panel changed during the wildly variable rotational speed changes.

As a result, our client experienced pain in her neck, shoulders, and upper body as the ride was operating. During the ride she tried every possible way to get the operator's attention, because of the serious pain she was experiencing. But, the operator was laughing hysterically and playing very loud music and did not respond to her.

After exiting the ride, she described her body as almost numb and that she could not feel her legs. She was examined in the emergency room where the medical personnel told her she was describing a feeling similar to a "stinger" as football players report after being hit hard.

Our contention was that the traveling carnival show, through its agents and employees, in reckless disregard of the consequences, operated the ride in an unsafe fashion in a manner not contemplated by the manufacturer.

The manufacturer's operating instructions detailed specific steps to follow to safely operate the machine. For example, the operating instructions provided: "Once everyone is positioned safely, press the ride "ON" button which starts the main electrical motor and accelerates the ride to the ... speed of 24 RPM's. When the seats have raised off the floor to their top position hold the button for about 10 seconds, then let go of the button. The ride will now coast [and] after a short time ... [the rider] will float back down to the floor." — This would result in a thrilling ride, but not the violent repetitive rapid up-and-down motion created by the ride operator.

The traveling carnival show ride operator exceeded the design tolerances of the equipment, causing the riders to move up and down in rapid succession instead of slowly floating up and then slowly down as intended. The riding experience as described by our client illustrated a practice of operation at odds with the manufacturer's operating instructions, and this operation put the plaintiff in a situation likely to cause injury, and it did in fact result in serious injury in this instance.

The ASTM Standards on Amusement Rides and Devices - Sixth Edition 2000 establishes that: "Each owner/operator of an amusement ride or device shall read and become familiar with the contents of the manufacturer's recommended operating instructions and specifications .... Each owner/operator shall prepare an operating fact sheet [that is] made available to each ride or device operator .... The owner/operator shall provide training for each ride or device operator and attendant of an amusement ride or device."

Additionally, we argued that riders were not warned regarding the potential risk of injury associated with the ride, either when operated normally, or in a dangerous abnormal fashion as occurred in this instance, nor were proper safety instructions posted at the ride consistent with safe amusement ride and device safety practices.

A sign being used by the carnival informed patrons with existing and pre-existing medical conditions that it was not recommended for them to experience the ride, but there was no information that informed riders not having the listed conditions they were also subject to a risk of injury. There was no warning of what could happen if the ride were operated in the manner that it was operated in this instance.

In short, we contended that the operator failed to follow critical safe operating procedures, was improperly trained, or made a conscious decision not to follow procedures, and acted with willful disregard of rider safety.

We were able to establish that the injury to our client was preventable and that the failures of the traveling carnival show directly caused our client's injuries. The case thereafter settled for a confidential sum.

I included this case because it illustrates that if machinery is not operated in a safe manner as intended by the manufacturer, injuries can and do occur. The type of machine may be different in each case, but the principle of law is the same whether the machine is an amusement ride, a fuel dispensing valve, a crane, excavation equipment, a rowboat, a tanning bed, a tractor and trailer combo, a motorboat – you name it. We have handled cases involving all such devices. Sometimes the operators have been reckless, sometimes inattentive, and sometimes intoxicated.

Up to this point we have focused on the mistakes, negligence, or recklessness of people who have caused an accident or injury. But people who are injured can make mistakes that jeopardize their legal rights *following their injury* if they don't have sound legal advice. That is the subject of the next chapter, Avoidable Mistakes. In it we examine "avoidable mistakes" from the perspective of the injured party and explain why it is critical following an injury incident to have legal counsel to help avoid such mistakes.

Chapter Eleven

~Avoidable Mistakes~

Avoidable mistakes. – Avoidable mistakes are what one might call unforced errors in baseball. If not vigilant, avoidable mistakes can worm their way into cases to sabotage the injury victims and interfere with their otherwise obtaining good outcomes. In this chapter, I share with you a number of common mistakes that people all too frequently make that can significantly diminish their chances of winning at trial – and offer ways to avoid them.

The first way a case can be significantly harmed is by hiring a lawyer who recommends or directs his or her client to a specific doctor. This is unacceptable.

Imagine the skepticism you would feel if you were serving on a jury and heard that there was a deal between a lawyer and a doctor. Just as going to an attorney who connects a client with a "special" doctor is a prime way to harm a case, so too is going to a doctor who connects the patient up to a "special" attorney. Highly unethical.

Our view is that when people are hurt or ill they need to seek out sound medical advice. From a medical standpoint, and a lawsuit perspective as well, neither a nurse practitioner nor a chiropractor is equipped to offer the best medical advice. Moreover, only a medical doctor can testify to a medical opinion in court (nurse and chiropractor testimony is largely restricted in court), which is important if the case goes to trial.

We *never* refer our clients to doctors. Instead we encourage people to think of their health first, and to look within their insurance policies for a capable medical doctor who is covered by their policy to treat them and help them regain their health.

Second, people can harm their cases by not accurately telling their doctor the history of their injury, or by telling the doctor a history of their health that is easily contradicted by the patients' medical records. Similarly, it is a mistake to fail to tell the attorney about past medical history.

Everyone, except perhaps a newborn, will have a pre-injury incident medical history. Frequently, this past history will include a prior injury involving a part of the body hurt in the current collision or injury incident. From a legal perspective this is not a big deal.

But, attorneys need to know exactly what went on in their clients' past medical history so that they can present an honest and straightforward case to the jury. Doctors also need an accurate history from their patients in order to supervise patient care. If a doctor is misled, even due to simple carelessness, it can lead to the wrong medical diagnosis or prognosis. If an attorney is misled, and then unwittingly misleads a jury, the outcome can similarly lead to a bad case result.

As an aside, in our experience, few people set out to fabricate or misrepresent their medical history (if we find that a client has done so *they do not remain* our clients). Rather, mistakes flow mostly from unconsciously exaggerating, being ashamed to admit something in their past, or the result of poor memory.

When our clients answer written questions under oath called interrogatories, we remind them to be accurate, truthful, and complete in their responses. We may ask them to review their own medical records.

When our clients must answer questions verbally under oath in a deposition, we remind them of the same need to be accurate, truthful, and complete in their responses, and again suggest that they review their records.

Another unfortunate mistake that can unnecessarily impede a case occurs when clients are not accurate about their activity levels. Defense teams often conduct video surveillance of the injury victim and through that surveillance they know what that person's true activity level is. Injury victims should not think they can hide information from their attorney, the judge, or the jury about their true activity level.

Defense teams also conduct social media surveillance. A fair way to look at social media is to imagine walking around surrounded by a four-sided cardboard box. On that cardboard box are posted (some by the owner of the box and some by "friends" of the owner) photos as well as little messages. We might think that some of these photos and messages are personal and not visible to the world, but courts can compel that the defense team be given access to these messages. Pretty frightening, right?

When a person gets hurt in an accident, that social media box goes to court with them. When a person testifies about how much their knee hurts after it got rammed into the dashboard, the jury can see the photos on the side of the social media box showing that person dancing or playing basketball. Typically, those photos don't show the pain the person endured while engaging in these activities.

The defense team will search every corner of the internet trying to find things out about an injury victim. They'll know everything about a person's Twitter and Facebook comments.

Armed with this information, the defense attorney will ask the injured party questions under oath in a deposition or at trial trying to pin them down about particular incidents which they know can be challenged with the social media information they have amassed. Once the injured party testifies, the attorney will use social media photographs and postings to attack the testimony.

Let's set surveillance issues aside for a moment and discuss the mechanics of how a deposition works. Giving testimony under oath at a deposition may seem daunting. Depositions usually occur at an attorney's office with a court reporter taking down everything said. The witness swears under oath to be truthful.

The defense attorney, whether mean or ingratiatingly kind, presents a real threat. Questions are designed to trap witnesses. However, *our team works very hard to help our clients get through the process*, to know what to expect, and to be comfortable and confident in responding. Our advice is simple: our clients are to listen to their attorney, follow their attorney's advice, and listen to the questions and answer them truthfully.

Our practice is to get our clients into the office in advance of a deposition and give them a thorough opportunity to prepare. Sometimes we have them watch videos of a deposition, and sometimes we go through a mock question-and-answer session so that they begin to feel what it's like to have to answer questions under pressure.

The mock question and answer sessions will include someone acting the part of a mean defense counsel, and also a very nice and polite defense counsel, because sometimes politeness can catch a person off guard.

Also, we help put our clients at ease by assuring them that during the deposition, their attorney will be present as an advocate to object when necessary, or otherwise ease them through the process. Getting our clients ready to sit for a deposition takes a bit of work, but it is time well spent, and countless times we have had our clients thank us for working to get them prepared.

Another way people can unwittingly harm their case is to, without reason, fail to follow their doctor's advice. For example, if a doctor prescribes physical therapy or a particular medication, it's not appropriate to ignore the doctor.

Now, if taking prescribed medication makes a person nauseous, the thing to do is to tell the doctor and ask for a new medication, not simply ignore the recommendations of the physician.

If physical therapy causes pain, a person needs to tell the therapist, and ask if a different, gentler approach can be taken. Stopping therapy without explanation gives an opening to the defense team to claim that the patient is not cooperating and not trying to get healthy.

Lastly, there is a type of error which I would categorize as a "forced error" in some respects. That is the error of speaking with and giving a statement to the insurance company representative for the party who may need to be sued for causing the injury.

Insurance adjusters are out to trick and trap an injury victim if at all possible. One can never go wrong by consulting an attorney first if an insurance adjuster seeks a statement. If an adjuster calls and tries to force a person to commit the mistake of giving them a statement, the best response is to indicate a desire to seek legal counsel before committing to giving a recorded statement.

Common Thread

The common thread in all these mistakes has to do with honesty. Always remember that "honesty is the best policy". Whoever said that was surely a genius.

Being painted as a liar by a defense attorney at trial can have calamitous consequences on a person's injury case. While meticulously honest people still run the risk of being painted as liars by an unscrupulous defense attorney, the goal is to make it extremely hard for the defense to paint a client as a liar, and for the jury to shrug it off if it is attempted at trial.

One often hears the phrase "the truth will set you free". What is it about the truth that makes it so powerful? If you haven't thought of truth as powerful, take a moment to do so.

Every case I have discussed thus far, and the successful outcomes achieved in those cases, depended on uncovering the truth. The solution for avoiding the missteps that lead people to harm their own case is, in almost every instance, to be honest. People who tell the truth respect their legal team, *respect themselves*, respect the court and respect the jury.

"For every good reason there is to lie, there is a better reason to tell the truth." - Bo Bennett. The truth is always easy to remember. Most of the mistakes or unforced errors noted in this chapter can be avoided by simply being truthful. Had a past accident or a past injury? Not a problem. The law provides that a person can recover damage for new harm to old injuries.

Forgot to file tax returns and worried it will hurt a wage loss claim? The solution is to file late tax returns. Filing late tax returns is certainly something people on a jury can appreciate. Many people who are incapacitated due to an injury get behind in filing taxes.

People who are truthful don't need to exaggerate. If there are things that a person can absolutely not do, it's perfectly fine to say, "I can't do these things." But if there are things a person can do, but they do it slower, or they feel a lot of pain when they do it, the proper response is to say "these things cause me a lot of pain, I have to slow down, I have to take breaks." Simple rule: be truthful and accurate; don't exaggerate.

One needs a guide to climb the highest mountains.

If someone you know needs guidance as a result of any injury incident, feel free to give them this book. It is not possible in this space to enumerate every danger lurking under every litigation rock, but here are some additional pointers, some of which are rephrased points already made in this chapter:

- Follow the advice of your doctors and work hard to regain your health.
- Be cautious about speaking to insurance claim people (your health insurance claim people included) without first obtaining legal advice.
- Keep everything pertaining to your case (bills, police reports, medical reports) in a box or envelope that you can take to your attorney.
- Hire a Board Certified Civil Trial Attorney.
- Select an attorney with an honest and ethical reputation.

- Select an attorney who will listen to you and care about you.

- Select an attorney who can explain the law to you in a clear, concise manner.

- Find an attorney who will communicate regularly with you and return your phone calls.

- Contact an attorney early enough so that he or she will be able to help preserve evidence, locate witnesses, and take measurements and photographs.

David W Holub

Chapter 12

~The Eye of The Hurricane~

I mentioned in the introduction that I would explain what it is like to be in the courtroom. To me it is very calming.

When I say to people that "when I am in trial it is a very calming time for me" most of them are perplexed by the statement. But, I mean precisely that.

When I am working on a trial I am actually working close to 80 hours per week during the week leading up to the trial. I am doing all the things I would ordinarily do on all my clients' cases during a normal 40-hour week. Then for the second 40 hours that I cram into the work week, I'm doing all the special preparation work that needs to be done to be successful at trial.

You don't just walk into the courtroom without preparation and expect to win. I hope the case discussions in the earlier chapters made this clear. Winning without preparation *never* happens. Typically, preparation time takes place in the evening after normal 8:00 to 5:00 business hours. But usually, I am at my creative best working on Saturday and Sunday.

The reason trial time is so calming though is that *during trial* I can jettison the 40-hour work week that is normally spent on cases that are not on trial. I have the luxury when I'm in trial of telling people "I can't get back to your phone call or respond to your email because I'm in trial". It's like being in the eye of a hurricane. A lot is going on around you, but right where you're standing it's calm.

That's not to say that during the trial week we only work from the time the courthouse opens at 8:30 a.m. until the time the courthouse closes at 4:30 p.m. We actually work late into the evening on most days we are in trial. The reason is that, even though we have prepared for each day of trial, we have to readjust our approach when things change or do not go quite as anticipated.

For example, let's assume that we plan to put two witnesses on the stand regarding medical-related issues. At the end of the first day, the first of the two planned witnesses has testified, was a great witness and did extremely well. That night we have to re-evaluate. Do we really want to put on the second witness since the first one made all the points we needed to make? That evaluation takes time because a lot must be considered.

Each time you put a witness on the stand you place that witness's testimony in the record, but you also expose that witness to cross-examination by the other side. Let's assume for example that your first witness made all the points you need to make in the trial, and no one laid a glove on that witness during cross-examination. Is that extra bit of information that you can get into evidence with the second witness worth allowing that witness to be exposed to cross-examination if harmful information might be brought out by the opposing party and end up harming your case? That is a judgment call.

That decision requires going through notes to make sure that the key points you needed to make were actually made in a persuasive way. It requires you to look through your notes as to what exhibits were admitted and which exhibits were excluded. Perhaps there's a trade-off, you need to make a couple extra points to help your case, but the witness that could make them could also make your case look bad if that witness does poorly on cross-examination. Decisions like this take time to make. Then, if you choose to drop a witness, you have to contact other witnesses and move them up in the lineup. That itself takes time.

A trial is like a Shakespeare play or a Rodgers and Hammerstein musical. The only difference is it hasn't been written yet. You have an outline of the play or musical. You know what you want to put on the stage, but no lines have been written. Oh yes, you might have an outline of what you expect witnesses will say, but nothing has actually been committed to a script like it would be in a play or musical.

You basically orchestrate the witnesses and exhibits and evidence that you want to put on the stage and then you wrestle with the opposing party and you wrestle with the judge in order to determine how the play unfolds. You obviously want it to unfold in the way most favorable to you and your client, but there are many variables that you cannot control.

It is also a little bit like chess. Sometimes you make a move and regret doing so. Sometimes you make a move knowing that it will lead to a piece being turned over, but you make it anyway because it lures your opponent into a trap from which they cannot escape.

So, during the time that trial is proceeding, your attention is not divided, but it's solely focused on the task at hand. That has a very calming effect.

Chapter 13

~Expectations~

Though you try your best to make sure the trial unfolds in the way most favorable to your client, not everything always works out as you would like. Sometimes things go wrong when you least expect it.

You can run through witness preparation with your client several times before trial. During that preparation, the client does exactly what you expect in terms of being polite and responsive to questions, and you anticipate that exact same behavior at trial when on the witness stand and sitting in front of a jury. But that isn't what happens.

When a witness is put on the witness stand at trial who fails to perform exactly as you anticipate, sometimes all you can do is improvise. I've had clients who get that deer in the headlights look as soon as you ask them to state their name. All of a sudden they can't seem to remember their name. If you ask them to describe how they felt right after they suffered an injury, they look at you and say "I hurt all over". When you ask them to be more descriptive, they simply repeat the same sentence.

Before trial when you went through things with your client, he was perfectly able to describe his pain and identify the part of the body experiencing the pain, but no longer is that possible. It's as if you're looking at someone who should be photographed and have his picture put next to the phrase "brain freeze" in a dictionary.

Not to worry. Things happen. Half of case preparation is done so that when it comes time to improvise, it appears to be effortless. There are many ways you can shake people out of their brain freeze mode.

Often, I try to do it with humorous questions. For example, I will ask a parent who is freezing up on the witness stand, "how long have you known your daughter?" The witness is usually quiet for a minute and then starts to laugh and says "well I obviously have known her since she was born." That seems to help loosen a witness up a bit.

But sometimes a witness examination remains like pulling teeth no matter what we do. In such cases, we work with them as best we can to get the necessary information in front of the jury, even when it does not go as smoothly as we had hoped. Maybe it means asking the court for a short recess. Maybe it means asking permission to approach the witness and hand them an exhibit.

Even when we do mock trial exercises where we have our clients answer questions before several members of our team, it somehow doesn't seem to be the same for some people as a live jury in an official courtroom. When you're in a courtroom and there's a real court reporter present, a microphone, and a bunch of people looking at you, including one high up on a bench wearing a black robe, it can be a challenging time to keep calm and to think and answer questions. It can also be an emotional time, since talking about injuries tends to bring up strong emotions.

What we normally find is that the people who freeze up, often are freezing up because the memories they are asked to tell us about (and to disclose to strangers) can be quite emotionally painful. They are afraid of breaking down and tearing up. They freeze instead.

They don't want to be embarrassed in front of other people and they think that by crying or breaking down they will be embarrassed. This type of "fear of displaying emotion" freeze we can usually address and work out in advance, however.

We realize that reliving a traumatic event can be extremely difficult. It is something that we anticipate and try hard to help clients work through well before they take the witness stand. Sometimes it requires asking clients to write down their feelings. Sometimes it requires just sitting and listening quietly while they work through their story a few times to the point that even if something is not comfortable, it is doable.

This brings me to my closing point. People who do not want to work hard on their own case, may not really want to go to trial. Let that sink in for a moment.

We *work very hard* to try to get the best result at trial or by settlement before trial, if a fair settlement can be struck. And, we expect our clients to work hard too. Of course, we do not expect catastrophically injured clients to do more than they are physically and mentally able to do.

But, if we ask clients to come in on the weekend and go over their testimony, we expect them to do it. If we ask clients to stay late after a full day of trial to work on some other aspect of the trial for the next day in the courtroom, we likewise expect our clients to make arrangements to be able to do that.

If we ask our clients to help us go through their medical bills and records, or to help identify witnesses who can tell about their life before and after they were injured we expect it to be done. Any clients who think they can hand over a case to an attorney and not put in the time and effort necessary to get a good result will only get a good result by sheer luck.

I have tried many cases. I've won many cases. And, a few times I've lost cases. I always immediately forget the ones I lose. Perhaps in the cases I've lost, luck was involved on behalf of the other party, but I know for the cases we've won we didn't depend on luck.

As Abraham Lincoln said, "Give me six hours to chop down a tree and I will spend the first four sharpening the axe." We mean it when we say that we work very hard to try to get the best result at trial, or by settlement before trial if a fair settlement can be struck.

Close to 97% of all civil cases in the United States settle before trial. Settling is easy if a person is prepared to take less than what is fair and reasonable. A person can easily settle a claim for next to nothing without hiring an attorney.

What is hard is extracting the best settlement. We have found over the years that the way to get the best settlement is to make certain our opponents know that we will not hesitate to take a case to trial if a fair offer is not forthcoming. Our opponents know we have well sharpened our axe and are ready to step into the courtroom swinging if a fair settlement cannot be reached.

A key reason a person needs an experienced and skilled trial lawyer who is ready and willing to go to trial is to increase their odds of obtaining a fair and full value settlement. I have never met a client who says, "no matter what the offer is I want to take my case to trial." Nearly every client instead says, "I would prefer not to go to trial if possible, but I need full compensation for what has happened to me; can you help me get there?" The answer in most cases is yes, unless of course the client *comes to us too late* and has already made a number of unintentional mistakes, which put that goal beyond reach.

While we do expect our clients to help us, the collaborative effort is one where we do the heavy lifting. For example, in nearly all cases the court expects the parties to complete mediation before being assigned to the court's trial calendar. A mediation is an opportunity for the parties to get together and discuss, in a neutral setting, the possibility of settlement. The neutral mediator is an experienced and respected attorney that both sides agree to use as their go-between.

When our clients' cases are ordered to mediation, we will meet with the client ahead of time and discuss in great detail what to expect out of the mediation process in their particular case. We explain that whatever is said privately to the mediator cannot be disclosed to the other side without permission. We help our clients understand that emotions can get in the way of settlement, such as when a plaintiff in an accident case is wanting to see the defendant punished for wrongdoing. We work through these issues with our clients ahead of time so they are ready to go through the mediation process and are prepared to try to arrive at a mutually-agreeable settlement.

While our clients must participate in mediations, answer questions in a deposition, and otherwise help us gather evidence to support their claims, the collaborative effort remains one where we do the heavy lifting. But, that means our clients *must be prepared to stay engaged* in the process and be willing to listen to our advice.

"Hard work spotlights the character of people: some turn up their sleeves, some turn up their noses, and some don't turn up at all." – Sam Ewing.

This book in many ways has been about the subject of TRUTH. Mr. Ewing's statement about hard work is of course *true*. When we work to help our clients, we roll up our sleeves. Whether it is helping one family get justice in the courtroom or helping 375 families in a subdivision recover from a flood, we turn up our sleeves.

Chapter 14

~The Truth is Out There~

A Need Arises

It's 9:00 p.m. and you're worried. Your husband should have been home two hours ago. You've tried to call him, but no answer. Another hour goes by. Then your phone rings. You glance down, it's your husband calling. But the voice on the other end is not your husband's. You hear, "Ma'am, this is Lieutenant Smith, your husband has been in a serious car accident, could you come to the hospital please."

Your heart is racing. You can't think straight. Your emotions are all over the place. You have a thousand questions. You make it to the hospital. Once there you rush to the emergency room front desk. The receptionist directs you to the third floor. The police lieutenant who spoke to you on the phone is there waiting for you.

A drunk driver collided with your husband's car. Both cars were destroyed in the collision. And your husband is in critical condition. You arrive just in time to see him before the doctor wheels him into surgery.

He has multiple fractures, a collapsed lung, head trauma…plus scores of lacerations all over his body, but he's alive. The driver of the other car, the one that hit him, is unconscious and it's undetermined if he will survive.

Your husband's life will be different. At least for the foreseeable future. He will require physical therapy, rest, pain management, and weekly doctor's checkups. Your daily routine will need to be adapted to account for your husband's various appointments.

Ready for Battle

Scenarios like these occur every day all across the United States. Lives are upended. And yes, drunk drivers are a public menace. But we believe, like Rev. Dr. Martin Luther King, Jr., that truth "will have the final word."

Such cases pose a difficult legal challenge sometimes, because while fault is frequently clear, a person who is irresponsible and drives drunk is also statistically likely to be financially irresponsible and have no insurance.

In such a situation we inquire to see if the injured person purchased uninsured and underinsured motorist (UIM) insurance coverage. This coverage protects the victim when the party who caused the collision has insufficient or no insurance.

In cases where there is no liability insurance and no UIM coverage, or inadequate insurance, the next step is to investigate who served the alcohol. Was the drunk driver at a wedding, party, bar, or tavern? Was the person served while observed to be intoxicated? Cases where proof of serving alcohol is important must be investigated quickly before memories fade and evidence disappears.

So, in cases like this, when family members call us about a drunk driver who collided with their husband, wife, son or daughter and caused an accident, we immediately begin the process of investigating the matter once hired. We ask a lot of questions. We obtain medical records. We acquire the police report and other information that would help support their claim.

But what if the driver of the oncoming vehicle wasn't drinking, what if they were using a cell phone to text or check social media? What if they were applying makeup or fiddling with their navigation system? What if they had a history of reckless driving? Name the circumstance; we have likely seen it before.

We've handled many cases over the years where the defendant driver was not just careless or negligent, but reckless. Maybe it is someone with a long history of moving violations. Might be speeding violations, running red lights, driving while suspended, or driving while under the influence. By a long history I don't mean just one or two tickets, I mean dozens of citations. Maybe the defendant driver even holds licenses in multiple states hoping to spread the large number of citations over multiple state records so as to avoid a license suspension.

Dangerous or reckless drivers almost invariably insist when testifying under oath to having had the right-of-way, or to having had the green light "when the light was last checked", or "the light was yellow as I was approaching so I knew when I went through the intersection it still must've been yellow", or "this other driver who left the scene didn't leave me enough room", or "someone waved me through". In such situations it is critical to identify witnesses quickly and get their observations pinned down. Countless times we have found that witnesses tagged by police as having very little information, actually have very important information critical to the case when we speak with them.

Trust in the Truth

When injured people are working through the process of selecting the right attorney, it can be frustrating. They're in pain. They're angry. And, information, as well as misinformation, is coming at them fast and from every direction, such as social media, newspaper ads, phonebook ads, TV ads, billboards, and those internet ads that stalk people from website to website, and follow them on their mobile devices (the dark side of the digital age).

If you are like most people, what you really want is someone you can trust, who understands what you are going through, and is willing to help and do the heavy lifting needed to make a financial recovery and who has the experience and track record as an advocate to go the distance, so that when you are told that things will be okay, you can feel confident that things indeed will get better.

We get it. This chapter paints a picture of what every new client call is like from our side. Callers want an attorney who will listen. An attorney who will point them in the right direction and tell them the steps they need to take to ready themselves for a legal fight.

The truth is out there, but the caller needs someone to find it; to fight for it. They want an attorney who is experienced with their type of injury or claim. They want a trustworthy lawyer, with a legal team that will take the time to care about them as a person first, and a case second. They want someone on their side fighting for truth and working hard to right the wrongs they have suffered.

Our goal at The Law Offices of David W. Holub is for all of our clients to know that we are there for them, fighting for them, defending them, educating them, and keeping them in the loop on their cases.

We invite you to make use of the large volume of information on our website www.davidholublaw.com.

We are *constantly updating* the website with video clips, and informational posts. You can search the website by navigating to the bottom of any page and selecting "search site" in the lower left column on the page.

Below are just a few remarks on our website, others can be found at…

https://www.davidholublaw.com/testimonials/

"[Website is] very useful …."
-Pamela H.

"The website is very informative … people [should see it] before making their … choice of attorney."
-George E.

"[W]ebsite is very beneficial … the articles and videos helped [me] to understand who will be representing [me] … ."
-Nicole C.

"Very satisfied … [website was] helpful!"
-Cynthia G.

David W Holub

About the Author

David W. Holub was admitted to practice before the Indiana State and U.S. Federal District Courts, Southern and Northern Districts of Indiana, in 1982. He was admitted to practice before the Supreme Court of the United States in 1995. He is also admitted to practice before the U.S. Federal District Court in the Northern District of Illinois.

Education: Olivet College (B.A. Magna Cum Laude, 1979); Valparaiso University (J.D. 1982). Associate Editor, Valparaiso University Law Review, 1981-1982.

Publications and Presentations:
- Seminar Moderator, What Civil Court Judges Want You to Know (NBI, October, 2017).
- Co-Author (with Katelyn Holub), Television and Furniture Tip-Over Cases, 38 Verdict 2 (2017).
- Speaker, Television and Furniture Tip Over Claims, (ITLA, May 2017).
- Speaker, Proving Pain, Suffering, and More in Personal Injury Litigation (NBI, Sept. 2016).

- Speaker, Advanced Issues in Personal Injury Litigation (NBI, December 2014).
- Speaker, Advanced Civil Litigation Skills in Indiana (NBI, Sept. 2015).
- Speaker, In the Trenches: Hearsay, Email, Business Records and Social Media (NBI, August, 2014).
- Speaker, Litigating Insurance Coverage Claims from Start to Finish (NBI, December, 2012).
- Speaker, Medicare Set-Asides in Personal Injury Litigation (NBI, October, 2011).
- Speaker, The Ambulance Intersection Case (ITLA, April 2010).
- Author, Preparing Dog Bite Cases, 28 Verdict 3 (2007).
- Author, The Rescue Doctrine, 30 Verdict 1 (2008).
- Co-author, Indiana Not-for-Profit Corporations: Standing to Maintain a Derivative Suit on Behalf of the Corporation, a Member's Suit to Enforce Membership Rights or a Citizen's Suit to Enforce Performance of Charitable Obligations, 25 Valparaiso University Law Review 249 (1991)

- Co-Author, Latent Heart Injury Following Vehicular Impact or Other Blunt Chest Trauma, 35 The Trial Lawyer's Guide 3 (Callaghan 1991).

- Author, The Contributory Negligence Defense as Applied Against Children in Indiana, 16 Valparaiso University Law Review 319-359 (1982).

Memberships: Lake County and Indiana State Bar Associations; The Association of Trial Lawyers of America; Indiana Trial Lawyers Association; The National Trial Lawyers; The American Association for Justice; "The Multi-Million Dollar Advocates Forum – The Top Trial Lawyers in America." ™

Certifications: Board Certified by the National Board of Trial Advocacy as a Civil Trial Advocate (1996).

The Law Offices of David W. Holub, P.C. provide a focused range of legal services and concentrate in personal injury and wrongful death litigation, including:
- Car, Truck, Semi-Truck Accidents
- Motorcycle, Bicycle and Pedestrian Accidents
- Railroad (Car – Train) Collisions
- Industrial and Construction Accidents

- <u>Medical Injury – Malpractice</u>
- <u>Medical Device and Medication Injuries</u>
- <u>Products Liability</u>
- <u>Wrongful Death</u>
- <u>Class Actions</u>
- <u>Premises: Slip and Fall, Dog Bite</u>
- <u>Insurance Disputes</u>

Moreover, this firm's practice includes the handling of claims stemming from many types of injuries and in particular is familiar with RSD (Reflex Sympathetic Dystrophy) and CRPS (Complex Regional Pain Syndrome) and many other less frequently encountered <u>medical conditions</u>. Further, David Holub is familiar with various product defects such as seatbelt and airbag defects, defective chainsaws, lawn mowers, power saws, defective medical devices, and other products.

The Law Offices of

David W Holub

8403 Merrillville Rd

Merrillville Indiana 46410

(219) 736-9700

www.DavidHolubLaw.com

David W Holub

Remember to…

Share This Book!

Share it with your friends!

Share it with your colleagues!

Share it on social media.

Share it using this hashtag...

#FightingForTruth

Remember to…

Share This Book!

Share it with your friends!

Share it with your colleagues!

Share it on social media.

Share it using this hashtag...

#FightingForTruth

www.ingramcontent.com/pod-product-compliance
Lightning Source LLC
Chambersburg PA
CBHW060545100426
42742CB00013B/2453